Say a Little Prayer

Say a Little Prayer

A JOURNAL

June Cotner

CHRONICLE BOOKS
SAN FRANCISCO

INTRODUCTION

Twenty years ago I started compiling a notebook of graces for my family. When my children were young, instead of using standard graces, I wanted to find more inspiring ways of expressing gratitude around the dinner table. When the same words are repeated again and again, praying becomes a mechanical act instead of a passionate connection with life and a higher spiritual power. On a trip west, my agent visited my home and looked through the devotions I had collected. She said it would have widespread appeal and would make a perfect book. She remarked that it would be stronger if I included pieces by lesser-known poets and writers, which was a brilliant suggestion. I placed a call for submissions and soon received an outpouring of prayers. *Graces* was published in 1994 and has now gone into thirty-seven printings. To my delight, I went on to create twenty-five more spiritual books. Finding moving prayers and inspirational poetry has become my life's work. More than 700 poets and writers have become regular contributors to my books, and this journal is a showcase of their most meaningful and encouraging words.

Whether you pray regularly or are somewhat new to prayer, *Say a Little Prayer* is a journal that will invigorate your spiritual life and deepen your connection to the Divine. We can all get busy in our lives and forget to pray, or sometimes we feel our spirituality needs rejuvenation. Using this journal on a regular basis will help you to make prayer the foundation of everyday life. While I pray daily, I still appreciate reminders that prompt me to pray for certain people, situations, and issues in my life and the world at large. That's why I need this journal, too, and why I am so pleased to have been given the opportunity to create it.

In *Say a Little Prayer*, you will find tips that will assist you in figuring out what works best for your prayer life; quotes about prayer and spirituality that will motivate you to pray daily; and fresh prayers covering many topics such as creating a spirit of praise and gratitude, facing life's challenges with courage, and living each day more consciously with kindness, compassion, and forgiveness. There is room to record all your thoughts and observations related to prayer and your evolving spiritual life. This journal will help you to keep track of what you wish to pray about and to list what you have prayed about.

To help you use this journal most effectively, I arranged the text so that some of the prayer prompts and themes build off earlier entries. If you prefer a serendipitous experience, you can open the journal to any page, and it will still work for you. The journal is designed with lots of space, so you can revisit topics again and see when a particular situation has been resolved or your prayers answered.

You might choose a specific place to pray, without distractions, and to write in your prayer journal. Keep a special pen with your journal so you need not search for one when you're ready to write. Many people find they like to pray at the same time each day, perhaps upon rising or before going to bed. If you're on the go a lot, you might prefer to take your journal with you, so you can use it throughout the day.

This journal is perfect for cultivating the spiritual discipline of praying. When we are in rhythm with our spiritual life, we find a meaning and purpose to existence that illuminates our smallest choices or actions and allows us to respond creatively and with discernment to life's challenges. My wish for you is that *Say a Little Prayer* will move you to pray more frequently and with more passion as you embark on your journey to enrich your prayer life.

**TAKE SOME TIME
TO REFLECT ON
YOUR PRAYER LIFE.**

What is working and
what is not? Write down
changes you would
like to make in order
to recapture passion in
your prayer life.

I am coming

IF YOU LIKE TO PRAY
UPON ARISING, THE
FACING PRAYER MAY
PUT YOU IN A PEACE-
FUL STATE OF MIND
AS YOU EMBRACE A
NEW DAY.

at daybreak, dear god,
fill me with your light.
let the sounds of gentle clouds
be like the sounds I make today.
remind me to say good morning to someone.
let me have strength
to face any adversity that may come my way
and let me face it with love.
or at least with patience.

MAGIE DOMINIC

**PRAY WITH A HEART
OF THANKFULNESS.**

Write down five things
you want to give thanks
for today.

 One single grateful thought raised to heaven is the most perfect prayer. 🙶

G. E. LESSING (1729–1781)

PRAY BEFORE EACH
MEAL. IF YOU ARE NOT
IN THE PRACTICE OF
SAYING GRACE, START
WITH SOMETHING
SIMPLE SUCH AS THE
FACING PRAYER.

Bless this meal, O God, we pray,
And bless us, too, throughout the day.
Keep us safe and close to you,
And kind in all we say and do.

THERESA MARY GRASS

**PRAY WITH A HEART
OF OPTIMISM.**

Write down five things
you want to pray about
today.

" If you believe, you will receive whatever you ask for in prayer. "

MATTHEW 21:22

May our family be blessed with comforts of the physical
　　　And riches of the spirit.
May our paths be lit with sunshine
　　　And sorrow ne'er darken our doors.
May our harvest be bountiful
　　　And our hearth ever welcoming.
May we celebrate together in times of joy
　　　And comfort one another in times of sorrow.
And mostly:
May we always stay together
　　　And share the laughter, the love, and the tears
　　　　As only family can.

DANIELLE BRIGANTE

VARY THE PLACES IN WHICH YOU PRAY.

If you pray in your bedroom, try praying in your kitchen. If you pray indoors, try praying in your backyard. After a few days of experimenting with new places to pray, write down what you discovered.

66 As often as you can, take a trip out to the fields to pray. All the grasses will join you. They will enter your prayers and give you strength to sing praises to God. 99

RABBI NACHMAN OF BRESLOV (1772–1810)

Thank you for our homes,
for the life we share together.
Help us to listen, love, and care,
To encourage one another.

THOMAS L. REID

**LIST FIVE PEOPLE
YOU WANT TO PRAY
FOR TODAY.**

Jot down your prayer
requests for each
person.

66 It is very important to pray for others, because when you pray for someone, an angel goes and sits on the shoulder of that person. 99

THE VIRGIN MARY AT MEDJUGORJE

Be with me as I enter Your presence.
Give me the patience and the stillness
to hear Your voice.
Fill me with Your spirit,
and help me to understand
what You want me to know.
Quieten my noisy head to make room
for what You want me to hear.
Grant me the wisdom to do Your will—
this day and in the days to come.
Bring me a blessing today
and help me to recognize it when I see it.

PHYLLIS K. COLLIER
(1939–2010)

BEFORE PRAYING TODAY, SIT IN SILENCE FOR TEN MINUTES AND BE READY TO RECEIVE GOD'S LOVE AND DIRECTION FOR YOUR LIFE.

Write down insights you experienced during this quiet time.

66 God speaks in the silence of the heart.
Listening is the beginning of prayer. 99

MOTHER TERESA (1910–1997)

Help me to remember
that in this world,
I am only visiting;
help me to have
the manners of a guest
and the hospitality
of family.

SALLY CLARK

THINK OF PLACES OR LANDMARKS YOU SEE EVERY DAY.

Whether it's a mountain, a playing field, or a billboard, make this object a memory-jogger for a prayer prompt. For example, when you see the mountain, ask for humility; when you see a playing field, ask for protection for your children; when you see the billboard, pray for world peace. Write down your ideas for other objects and prayer-prompt associations.

O God of whirling galaxies, rain forests and rivers, tides and thunderstorms, we've been too busy to notice how our choices affect our world. At last we're paying attention: You gave us a gift but we were careless and now it's broken. We gather today, repentant, hopeful, and determined to restore, cleanse, and bring new life to earth, wind, and creature. Let us share Your imagination; let us be Your fingers as we tend this gift, which holds and carries us all.

REV. J. LYNN JAMES

date /   /

**OFFER TO PRAY
FOR FAMILY AND
FRIENDS.**

Record your prayer
requests for them
here.

May my intuition lead me
through the choices of today.
May my loving heart guide me
and be the one to have first say.
May my body's strength support me
and hold all the ills at bay.
May my mind's meanderings calm me
and keep me balanced in every way.

KAY ELIZABETH

**VARY YOUR
PRAYER ROUTINE.**

Try praying at different
times of day. For exam-
ple, if you are rushed in
the morning, you might
find that evening prayer
works better for you. Or
you might find that you
prefer to pray during
a daily walk. After you
have tried a few changes
to your prayer routine,
write down what works
best for you.

date / /

66 Prayer is as natural an expression of faith as breathing is of life. 99

⬭ JONATHAN EDWARDS (1703–1758)

Today
grant me the ability to help myself
and to help others.
Let me be a light
for those who move in darkness.
Let me be a source of healing
for those that hurt.
Let me show the way
to those who are lost.
Let me forgive
those who are unforgiving.

CORRINE DE WINTER

66 Grant that I may not pray alone with the mouth; help me that I may pray from the depths of my heart. 99

MARTIN LUTHER (1483–1546)

**LIST WAYS YOU WANT
TO SEEK HARMONY
AND SPIRITUAL BAL-
ANCE IN YOUR HOME.**

Whatever is in harmony with you, O Universe,
is in harmony with me.
Whatever comes in due season for you
is not too early or too late for me.
What your seasons bring is fruit for me,
for all things come from you and return to you.

MARCUS AURELIUS

MEDITATIONS, BOOK IV, 23, TRANSLATED BY MARYANNE HANNAN

**LIST FIVE PEOPLE
YOU WANT TO PRAY
FOR TODAY.**

Jot down your requests
for each person.

To the Gardener of the World—
Thank you for arousing in us
a hunger to live,
for bringing us to rest
in the shade of your Tree of Life,
for awakening in us
the light of your promise,
for breathing into our weary limbs
your spirit of refreshment and renewal.

FR. JOHN B. GIULIANI

FIND OR CREATE SOME TRIGGERS THAT WILL REMIND YOU TO PRAY.

A trigger could be a sticky note on your bathroom mirror, an hourly alarm on your watch, or a small stone you carry in your pocket. List your triggers and your prayer associations for each trigger. For example, an hourly alarm can remind you to pray for your family. Feeling the small stone in your pocket could prompt you to express praise and gratitude.

66 Certain thoughts are prayers. There are moments when, whatever be the attitude of the body, the soul is on its knees. 99

VICTOR HUGO (1802–1885)

**DO YOU FEEL YOU ARE
HAVING A DIFFICULT
TIME WITH SOMEONE?**

Create a prayer asking
for help to bring more
wisdom, kindness,
and humility to your
relationship with this
person.

Let me recognize, O God,
the good in everyone.
Keep me from a critical attitude
and inspire me to be open to all.
Encourage me to learn from others' ways
and to share knowledge willingly.
Bless me with a heart that loves,
hands that reach out,
eyes that see the beautiful
and a voice that speaks of truth.

THERESA MARY GRASS

**THINK OF SOMEONE
WHO NEEDS A SPECIAL
PRAYER.**

Write down your prayer
for this person.

date / /

WHEN YOU SHOWER,
PRAY TO BE CLEANSED
OF ANY FEELINGS OF
ANGER, RESENTMENT,
OR REGRET.

Give us courage, gaiety, and the quiet mind.
Spare us to our friends, soften to us our enemies.
Bless us, if it may be, in all our innocent endeavors.
If it may not, give us the strength to encounter
that which is to come, that we be brave in peril,
constant in tribulation, temperate in wrath,
and in all changes of fortune and down to the gates
of death, loyal and loving one to another.

ROBERT LOUIS STEVENSON
(1850–1894)

**WRITE DOWN FIVE
THINGS YOU WILL
DO TO PRACTICE
COMPASSION AND
KINDNESS TODAY.**

66 Be kind, for everyone you meet is fighting a hard battle. 99

◯◯ **PLATO** (427–347 BC)

This day,
Let me be:
Ready at your beckoning
Faithful on my journey
Constant in my efforts
To be Your song.

MARY LENORE QUIGLEY

**MAKE LISTS TO KEEP
TRACK OF YOUR
PRAYER NEEDS.**

Your lists might include
prayers for those who
are ill, grieving the loss
of a loved one, or experi-
encing other difficulties.

Grant me sustenance
that I may share it.
Grant me light
that I may shine it.
Grant me hope
that I may accomplish it.
Grant me love that I may cherish it
this day and always.

KAY ELIZABETH

**WRITE DOWN THREE
THINGS YOU WANT TO
PRAY ABOUT TODAY.**

66 Prayer is not asking. It is a longing of the soul. It is daily admission of one's weakness. It is better in prayer to have a heart without words than words without a heart. 99

MAHATMA GANDHI (1869–1948)

THINK OF A FAMILY MEMBER WHO IS STRUGGLING.

Write down your prayer for this person.

Dear God, I pray for all the members of my family:
for those who are growing up,
that they may increase in wisdom and love;
for those facing changes, that they may meet them with hope;
for those who are weak, that they may find strength;
for those with heavy burdens, that they may carry them lightly;
for those who are old and frail, that they may grow in faith.

AUTHOR UNKNOWN

PRAY WITH A HEART OF GRATITUDE.

Write down five ways that you feel blessed.

66 Grow flowers of gratitude in the soil of prayer. 99

 TERRI GUILLEMETS

Help me to know where to be mentally
        to receive what You want to tell me.
Help me to do the right thing
        in all my life's quandaries and predicaments.
Show me the way out of the maze of my difficulties.
Help me to find the hidden opening in the brick walls.
If it doesn't go my way,
        give me the grace I'll need,
        or the imagination and fortitude to try another way.
Drop me a lifeline when I'm about to give up.

PHYLLIS K. COLLIER
(1939–2010)

THINK OF WAYS YOU CAN BECOME A FORCE FOR GOOD IN THE WORLD.

Try to do one small thing every day. It might be something as simple as greeting everyone with a genuine smile. Pray for divine guidance, and record your small actions here.

Let me leave margins of silence
around the activities of day,
letting You write down there
whatever it is You would say.

Then looking backward, I find,
no matter how much I revise,
it is in Your footnotes
that the heart of my life lies.

ELIZABETH SEARLE LAMB
(1917–2005)

**LIST FIVE PEOPLE
YOU WANT TO PRAY
FOR TODAY.**

Jot down your prayer
requests for each person.

66 Pray for your enemies, that they may be holy and that all may be well with them. And should you think this is not serving God, rest assured that more than all prayers, this is indeed the service of God. 99

FROM THE TALMUD

May I always see beauty in the world
And hear music every day.
May I know the touch of gentle hands
And walk the peaceful way.
May the words I speak be loving
And show concern and care.
May I be blessed with hope
And joy in all I say and do.

THERESA MARY GRASS

date / /

TAKE A FEW MINUTES TO THINK ABOUT WAYS YOU WOULD LIKE TO BECOME A BETTER PERSON.

What character traits would you like to improve? Record your ideas. Choose two of the most important ones and pray to commit to improving these traits.

 Pray as if everything depended on God.
Work as if everything depended on you. 99

SAINT IGNATIUS LOYOLA (1491–1556)

LIST WAYS IN WHICH
YOU CAN PRACTICE
KINDNESS AND LOVE
TOWARD OTHERS
TODAY, WHETHER
THEY BE FAMILY MEM-
BERS, CO-WORKERS,
OR EVEN STRANGERS.

At the end of the day,
write down the ways
your loving kindness
made a difference.

Enveloped in Your Light,
may I be a beacon to those in search of Light.
Sheltered in Your Peace,
may I offer shelter to those in need of peace.
Embraced by Your Presence,
so may I be present to others.

RABBI RAMI SHAPIRO

date / /

TRY THIS SIMPLE MEDITATION:

Find a place that is quiet. Sit in a comfortable position, either in a chair or on the floor, with your back and head straight. Close your eyes and focus on your breath. Close your mouth and relax your jaw as you breathe in and out through your nose. As you breathe out, exhale all stress and tension. As you breathe in, inhale a vision of lightness and serenity. Practice this meditation for about 10 to 20 minutes.

date   /   /

66 Prayer is when you talk to God; meditation is when you listen to God. **99**

DIANA ROBINSON

THINK OF WAYS YOU CAN SHARE YOUR SPIRITUAL EXPERIENCE WITH OTHERS WHILE STILL REMAINING HUMBLE.

Think about someone in your life who is spiritual and humble and who truly treats others with loving kindness. Pray to become more like this person.

In You through whom
all things speak,
use me please
to sing your song.

KATE ROBINSON

**PRAY TO BECOME
MORE CALM AND
CENTERED.**

List the ways you
struggle with things or
experience stress.

66 In all endeavors
Strive to celebrate
The spirit of the warrior . . .
Calm,
Centered,
Certain . . .
Whether tending to the flower garden
Or searching for the heart of the divine. 99

JO-ANNE ROWLEY

**LOOKING UP AT
THE SKY TONIGHT,
EXPERIENCE THE
WAYS IN WHICH YOU
FEEL CONNECTED TO
THE DIVINE.**

Breathe deeply and let
that connection spread
to people around the
world. Practice this on
multiple evenings, and
before going to bed,
record any thoughts
or reflections in your
journal.

Oh Great Mystery of Being,
Let my small story connect to your larger one.
May we breathe with one breath.
May we make this day holy together.

REV. NITA PENFOLD

**THINK OF SOME-
ONE THAT YOU HAVE
WRONGED.**

Create a prayer of
apology and record
it here.

66 Action flows from the spring of prayer.
May each word be honest.
May each touch be healing.
May each step be peace. 99

 EDWARD A. DOUGHERTY

PRAY THAT YOU WILL PAY ATTENTION TO MOMENTS OF INNER PEACE WHILE GOING ABOUT YOUR ROUTINE ACTIVITIES TODAY.

List three ways that you would like to bring a sense of sacredness to ordinary experiences.

God help us to live quietly
Amidst the clamor,
To find that slower pace
that gentler place.
Where our hearts can listen,
Where we can listen to
Our hearts.
Amen.

JIM CROEGAERT

**WHAT HAVE YOU
NOTICED ABOUT THE
PROGRESS OF YOUR
PRAYER LIFE?**

Take a few minutes to
record your thoughts
and reflections here.

66 One of the best ways to worship God is simply to be happy. 99

 TRADITIONAL HINDU SAYING

I know that at times I will be troubled,
I know that at times I will be belabored,
I know that at times I will be disquieted,
but I believe that I will not be overcome.
Amen.

JULIAN OF NORWICH
(1342–CA. 1419)

**MAKE PRAYER A DAILY
PART OF YOUR LIFE.**

List your plans for
today and recommit
yourself to pray
throughout the day.

Bless my time in darkness
that it may simply be
a waiting within
a chrysalis.

And I will emerge
anew
with the warmth of the sun
to dry my wings.

BARBARA DAVIS-PYLES

**THINK OF SOMEONE
WHO NEEDS A SPECIAL
PRAYER.**

Write down your prayer
for this person.

Imagine not that life is all doing.
Stillness, too, is life;
and in that stillness
the mind cluttered with busyness quiets,
the heart reaching to win rests,
and we hear the whispered truths of God.

RABBI RAMI SHAPIRO

date / /

PRAY WITH A HEART OF THANKFULNESS.

Write down five things you want to give thanks for today.

The light of God surrounds me;
The love of God enfolds me;
The power of God protects me;
The presence of God watches over me.
Wherever I am, God is.

AUTHOR UNKNOWN

66 So long as we enjoy the light of day may we greet one another with love.
So long as we enjoy the light of day may we pray for one another. 99

ZUNI BLESSING

May all I say and all I think
be in harmony with thee,
God within me, God beyond me,
maker of the trees.

CHINOOK PRAYER

**IN WHAT WAYS DO
YOU HAVE TROUBLE
FORGIVING YOURSELF?**

What are past actions
you regret or wish you
had handled differently?
Record your thoughts
here. Take some time and
pray to forgive yourself.
By forgiving yourself,
you can open the path-
way to forgive others for
their actions that have
hurt you.

I do not ask to walk smooth paths
nor bear an easy load.
I pray for strength and fortitude
to climb the rock-strewn road.

Give me such courage and I can scale
the headiest peaks alone,
And transform every stumbling block
into a stepping stone.

GAIL BROOK BURKET

66 Today you will witness countless miracles, starting with the sun's dawning. 99

CORRINE DE WINTER

**PRAY WHILE READING
THE NEWSPAPER.**

Write down the names
of three people who are
suffering, and pray for
their healing.

Steer the ship of my life, good Lord, to your quiet harbor, where I can be safe from the storms of sin and conflict. Show me the course I should take. Renew in me the gift of discernment, so that I can always see the right direction in which I should go. And give me the strength and the courage to choose the right course, even when the sea is rough and the waves are high, knowing that through enduring hardship and danger in your name we shall find comfort and peace.

BASIL OF CAESAREA
(CA. 330–379)

**HAVE YOU HAD
ANY ANSWERED
PRAYERS SINCE YOU
STARTED THIS
PRAYER JOURNAL?**

Take a moment to reflect
and write down your
answered prayers.

Lead us through
Our darkest night,
Give us wisdom,
Give us light.

May our blessings
Never cease,
Give us courage,
Give us peace.

CHARLES GHIGNA

**THINK OF SOMEONE
WHO HAS HURT YOU.**

Pray to forgive this
person.

66 The only way to reconcile yourself, make peace with yourself, make peace with your neighbor, make peace with God, find salvation, is to break through and love—to forgive and to love. You don't change the person you forgive. You change your own heart. 99

REV. FORREST CHURCH

**PRAY TO PROTECT
OUR SOLDIERS AND
CHAPLAINS FROM
HARM. PRAY FOR OUR
WORLD LEADERS.**

Help us to do our best—
to strive for justice and fairness
even when it seems the world around us
is mired in ancient antagonisms.
Lend us the wisdom to cherish each bridge
we're able to build, even when
they're neither as grand nor as wide
as the span of our dreams,
and grant us the grace to trust the future
to forgive us for the things we could not change
as it crosses the rivers we thought impassable.

PEG DUTHIE

> Trouble and perplexity drive me to prayer, and prayer drives away perplexity and trouble.

PHILIP MELANCHTHON

**PICK ONE PERSON TO
PRAY FOR THROUGH-
OUT THE DAY.**

Write down your prayer
for this person.

Let me be a light, O God,
That shines for all to see;
If someone needs to find the way,
an example may I be
Of love and kindness and brotherhood,
Of all that's gentle, of all that's good.

THERESA MARY GRASS

date / /

WHAT ARE SOME WAYS YOU FIND BEAUTY IN THE WORLD?

Record them here.

Let the beauty that we love be what we do. There are hundreds of ways to kneel and kiss the ground.

RUMI (1207–1273) TRANSLATED BY COLEMAN BARKS

PRAY WHEN RIDING AN ELEVATOR.

Ask God to bless those around you. Try this same exercise when you are traveling on a subway, a bus, a plane, or a ferry.

Bless to me, O God, the earth beneath my feet,
Bless to me, O God, the path whereon I go,
Bless to me, O God, the people whom I meet,
Today, tonight, and tomorrow.

CELTIC BLESSING

**HERE IS ANOTHER
SIMPLE MEDITATION:**

Find a quiet place. Sit in
a comfortable position,
either in a chair or on
the floor, with your back
and head straight. Close
your eyes and focus on
your breath. Close your
mouth and relax your
jaw as you breathe in
and out through your
nose. Find the stillness
in your breath and
rest within it. On each
exhalation, repeat aloud
the word "om" (rhymes
with "dome"), drawing
out the "o" sound and
the "mmm." Do your best
to relax and be as still
as possible during your
meditation. Practice this
meditation for about 10
or 20 minutes.

**HOW CAN YOU HELP
YOUR COMMUNITY?**

Write down your ideas
and pray for help in
making your vision
a reality.

God, on this day
I welcome you into my heart.
I ask you for the patience
and wisdom,
for the light and understanding
to help others, to help myself,
to allow me the strength
to make my life worthy and meaningful
as you have intended it to be.

CORRINE DE WINTER

**WRITE DOWN THREE
THINGS YOU WANT TO
PRAY ABOUT TODAY.**

66 Ask and it will be given to you; seek and you will find; knock and the door will be opened to you. 99

MATTHEW 7:7

May the spark of love
ignite my soul.
May the burning flame
of charity
inspire all my actions
so I become a light
to the lonely.
Like a candle
that brightens the night,
may I always lead others
to loving and peaceful havens
in our dark and restless world.

THERESA MARY GRASS

66 There is a sanctuary in your heart where the spirit always waits. 99

CORRINE DE WINTER

66 The greatest of all truths is that love never dies, that every act of love that we perform in this life is carried on into another life and passed on into another life. 99

REV. FORREST CHURCH

I am the Song that never ends
and I sing for you.
I am the Prayer that never ends
and I pray for you.
I am the Love that never ends
and I love you.

JOAN SHROYER-KENO

 The will of God can never lead you where the grace of God cannot keep you.

AUTHOR UNKNOWN

**TAKE OUT A FAVOR-
ITE PHOTO ALBUM
OR SCROLL THROUGH
PHOTOS ON YOUR
COMPUTER.**

Looking at the photos,
note the names of
precious loved ones in
your life and ask God
to bless them.

**PRAY FOR HARMONY
WITHIN YOUR FAMILY.**

Ask God for help in
sending your love and
forgiveness to your
parents, your siblings,
your children, and
everyone in your
extended family.

Gentle God, grant that at home
where we are most truly ourselves,
where we are known at our best and worst,
we may learn to forgive and be forgiven.

A NEW ZEALAND PRAYER BOOK

PRAY WHILE WALKING.

Begin with giving
thanks and praise. Pray
for the needs of people,
animals, and places you
see. Focus on spreading
loving peace with every
step you take.

66 Give thanks for unknown blessings already on their way. 99

NATIVE AMERICAN SAYING

PRAY FROM YOUR HEART. WRITE DOWN YOUR CONCERNS TODAY AND ASK FOR HELP IN PRAYER.

Are you sometimes frustrated with negative parts of your personality? The facing prayer is an excellent one to return to time and again. Take a few minutes to write about what you would like to improve before saying this prayer.

Just for today,
I will strive to recognize
The beauty within myself.
I will escape discouragement
And replace it with virtue.
I will offer compassion
And forgive my faults.
I will bury self-doubt
And plant seeds of optimism.
I will cast out bitterness
And treasure purity.
Today . . .
I will embrace every good thing
And surrender myself to God.

LESLIE A. NEILSON

**WHAT HAVE YOU
NOTICED ABOUT THE
PROGRESS OF YOUR
PRAYER LIFE?**

Take a few minutes to
record your thoughts
and reflections here.

**THINK OF A COUNTRY
THAT IS SUFFERING A
WAR OR A NATURAL
DISASTER.**

Create a prayer asking
God to send love to all
families who have lost
loved ones. Pray that
peace may come to their
country.

I pray today for
Those who are homeless to find shelter.
Those who are depressed to discover joy.
Those who are addicted to find release.
Those who are lonely to find a friend.
Those who are confused or lost to find a path.
Those who are heartbroken to know that it will pass.
Those who are sick to find healing.
Those who live in darkness to be covered in light.
Those who are dying to know that they have lived.
I pray today for peace where there is unrest,
for love to prevail over all.

CORRINE DE WINTER

**WRITE ABOUT AN AREA
IN YOUR LIFE WHERE
THERE IS CONFLICT.**

Pray for help in illumi-
nating this darkness
to bring peace to this
situation.

66 Go forth in every direction—for the happiness, the harmony, the welfare of the many. Offer your heart, the seeds of your own understanding like a lamp overturned and re-lit again illuminating the darkness. 99

THE BUDDHA (563–483 BC)

Grant me the ability to be alone;
May it be my custom to go outdoors each day
among the trees and grasses,
among all growing things
and there may I be alone,
and enter into prayer
to talk with the one
that I belong to.

RABBI NACHMAN OF BRESLAV
(1772–1811)

**PRACTICE MINDFUL-
NESS TODAY BY BEING
COMPLETELY IN TOUCH
WITH AND AWARE OF
THE PRESENT MOMENT.**

As a first step, many
people find that a
solitary, contemplative
walk lends itself to this
practice. After your walk,
record the thoughts,
feelings, and associations
that came up during
your mindfulness walk.
What sights, sounds, and
smells did you notice?

Be for us Light in all our darknesses.
Be for us Calm in every storm.
Be for us Stillness in our turmoil.
Let Your Grace now rest upon us.

DEBORAH GORDON COOPER

66 Just to be is a blessing. Just to be is holy. 99

RABBI ABRAHAM J. HESCHEL (1907–1972)

God grant me the serenity
to accept the things I cannot change,
courage to change the things I can,
and wisdom to know the difference.
Amen.

REINHOLD NIEBUHR
(1892–1971)

66 Just pray for a tough hide and a tender heart. 99

RUTH GRAHAM (1920–2007)

THINK OF SOMEONE WHO NEEDS A SPECIAL PRAYER.

Write down your prayer for this person.

Blessed are You, Beloved,
Who shows me the Way
and accompanies me on the journey.
May I live the day's unfolding with compassion
and foster faith in the One Who is all.

RABBI RAMI SHAPIRO

66 I believe that God is in me
as the sun is in the color and fragrance
of a flower—
the Light in my darkness,
the Voice in my silence. 99

HELEN KELLER (1880–1968)

THE AUTHOR OF THE
FACING PRAYER WAS
INSPIRED BY THE
POETRY OF WILLIAM
STAFFORD AND DEDI-
CATED THE PRAYER
TO HIM.

Today, see if you can
find a phrase, a short
sentence, or even a
thought to use in creat-
ing your own prayer.
Record the phrase and
your prayer here.

(FOR WILLIAM STAFFORD)

Divine One,
We live and breathe
Your great goodness.
Bless us
With your healing spirit.

Let It rest among us,
So that we may see
With restored vision
Ourselves,
The gift of life,
And our ride among the stars.

SHIRLEY KOBAR

**PRAY WITH A HEART
OF SERENITY**

Write down five
things you want to
pray about today.

66 Our prayers should be for blessings in general, for God knows what is good for us. 99

SOCRATES (469–399 BC)

God, let me see this world of mine
Through thankful eyes,
And see the good in even those
Whose actions I despise,
While in myself I learn to have
Simple humility,
And tolerance for all of those
Who don't agree with me.

HILDA LACHNEY SANDERSON

**LIST FIVE PEOPLE
YOU WANT TO PRAY
FOR TODAY.**

Jot down your prayer
requests for each person.

O God, help us not to despise or oppose
what we do not understand.

WILLIAM PENN
(1644–1718)

An authentic life is the most personal form of worship. Everyday life has become my prayer.

SARAH BAN BREATHNACH

PRAY WITH A HEART OF GRATITUDE.

Write down five ways you feel blessed.

Be thou a bright flame before me,
Be thou a guiding star above me,
Be thou a smooth path below me,
Be thou a kindly shepherd behind me,
Today—tonight—and forever.

ST. COLUMBA OF IONA
(AD 521–597)

date / /

LOOK BACK OVER YOUR WORDS AND REFLECT ON WHAT EFFECT KEEPING THIS PRAYER JOURNAL HAS HAD ON YOUR LIFE.

Write down some of your favorite exercises. Why were they effective for you? Pick out a few exercises that you found the most worthwhile and commit yourself to making them a permanent part of your life.

May we walk with grace
and may the light of the universe
shine upon our path.

66 Rejoice always; pray without ceasing; in everything give thanks 99

1 **THESSALONIANS** 5:16-18

ABOUT THE AUTHOR

June Cotner is the author or editor of twenty-six books, including the best-selling *Graces, Bedside Prayers,* and *House Blessings.* She has appeared on national radio programs and been featured in many national publications, including *USA Today, Better Homes and Gardens, Woman's Day,* and *Family Circle.* She teaches workshops around the country on a variety of subjects and lives in Poulsbo, Washington.

For more information, please visit www.junecotner.com.

ACKNOWLEDGMENTS

I would like to graciously thank all of the contributors who have allowed me the use of their words in this journal. In particular, Coleman Barks, Danielle Brigante, Sally Clark, Robert E. Collier for Phyllis K. Collier, Deborah Gordon Cooper, Jim Croegaert, Barbara Davis-Pyles, Corrine De Winter, Magie Dominic, Edward A. Dougherty, Peg Duthie, Kay Elizabeth, Charles Ghigna, Theresa Mary Grass, Fr. John B. Guiliani, Maryanne Hannan, Rev. Jo Lynn James, Shirley Kobar, Carolyn Lamb for Elizabeth Searle Lamb, Leslie A. Neilson, Rev. Nita Penfold, Mary Lenore Quigley, Thomas L. Reid, Kate Robinson, Jo-Anne Rowley, Hilda Lachney Sanderson, Rabbi Rami Shapiro, and Joan Shroyer-Keno.

Library of Congress Cataloging-in-Publication Data available.

ISBN: 978-1-4521-0232-0

Manufactured in China

Designed by Emily Dubin

10 9 8 7 6 5 4 3 2 1

Chronicle Books
680 Second Street
San Francisco, CA 94107
www.chroniclebooks.com